She Li'
Moments

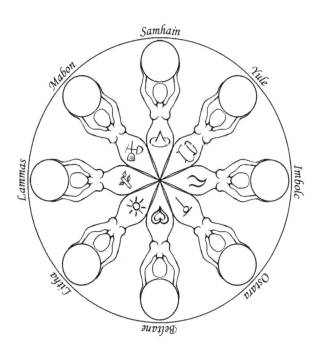

By Molly Remer, MSW, M.Div,
D.Min

brigidsgrove.com

She Lives Her Poems: Moments from a Year in the Forest

By Molly Remer, MSW, M.Div, D.Min

ISBN: 9781790721245

Published by: Brigid's Grove

brigidsgrove.com

With love to our patrons on Patreon.
Thank you for your support,
encouragement, and magic.

Introduction: Wild Snail Festivals

"Island living has been a lens through which to examine my own life...I must keep my lens when I go back... I must remember to see with island eyes. The shells will remind me; they must be my island eyes."

—Anne Morrow Lindbergh, *Gift from the Sea*

Each winter, we travel with our family to a small island in the Gulf Coast outside of Alabama and spend a month living on the beach. There is something about being on an island that quite literally transports you into another world. The sensation of stepping out, stepping off, and stepping *into* is palpable as we cross the bridge to the island and settle into the slow, quiet rhythm of island life, guided by the tides, the moon, and the rising and setting of the sun. Our sleep and waking schedules change. Our priorities shift. Our to-do lists become very short. While we enjoy a creative, home-based life and business at home in Missouri, there is something incredibly freeing, and clarifying, about laying everything aside and having the biggest item on the schedule be a long walk on the beach upon which we walk from two to five hours each day. We actually bring our business along with us in a travel trailer, so we aren't truly off work during this month, but instead of making everything as we go, we only sell the inventory we've already completed and brought with us, which leaves us with many extra hours a day compared to our work at home.

As I shed layers of myself at the beach, watching dolphins, running with my children, picking up shells, walking hand in hand with my husband into the setting sun, life feels simple, and what I need and want feels very clean and very clear. My intense self-motivation and drive softens, my itch to get more done and to make more lists fades away, and I am left with the core of myself and discover, anew, how very much I like her.

This year, the morning after we arrived at the island, my husband and I headed to our favorite part of the beach where the beachcombing is the best and the shells are the biggest. We were stopped on the road at a little guard tower and told we could not continue. When we inquired why, the sour-faced man told us with the smirk that the beach was "gone" and it had been destroyed in a hurricane last fall. He clearly took delight in breaking the news to us and very much enjoyed the act of turning us away.

We returned to our beach house in a state of confusion and shock. Our long walks on the beach, our hopes for the new treasures we would discover, the part of the island we so love and have so many happy memories of, all swept away. We walked on a different part of the island feeling a genuine sense of distress and grief. How could the beach just be gone? Does the island now just abruptly drop away into the sea? We feel a sensation that something had died. As we walk, we decide that the gift in this disappointment is that we will now explore and learn from different parts of the island than we are used to and that we can find new things to do and love while here, that we need to release our attachment to past visits and the ways things used to be and enjoy discovering what is right here, right now. But, then I say that I do not want to rush to make it all better, but instead I would like to just sit with and acknowledge the grief, and loss, and disappointment, rather than hurrying to turn everything into a lesson.

We walk in silence for a time and then realization dawns. There is no way the beach we long for can actually be gone. There is still a road visible headed in that direction and many dump trucks and earth-moving equipment driving back and forth. That part of the beach is damaged, we realize, but the facts we can see with our own eyes do not point to the total erasure of it as suggested by our power hungry little friend in his road-blocking shed.

Back in the beach house we google to discover that yes, the beach sustained significant hurricane damage in the fall and restoration efforts are underway. The correct description from the guard should have been that the beach is "closed for restoration" and not "gone." We continue to try to accept our gift of making new discoveries in the face of disappointment, but a few days later we decide to ask at the rental company if there is a way we can still go to the closed part of the island. They are able to give us a pass to enter it, and so, in fact, we *are* able to walk on our favorite part of the beach after all. The parking lot is damaged, but the beach itself is still very much there and very much alive.

This is a new gift, I muse. Rather than accepting our initial grief and disappointment, we *tried again.* Sometimes, you do not actually need to accept no for an answer, but you can push a little more and get what you want. What if we had just turned away in grim acceptance and gone with the flow instead of twisting a little harder and asking for what we want? I try to reconcile the two lessons—the letting go *and* the pushing, our refusal to let go. And then, a third lesson: *not everything has to be a lesson*, sometimes things just *are.*

My favorite shell in the world is from a moon snail. Round, smooth, and beautiful, curling in a wave to a perfect tiny spiral in the center, with colors ranging from brown to pale blue, many of the moon shells we find are small, the size of a quarter or smaller. My holy grail (holy snail) is a palm-sized moon shell that will fill my hand. In the morning as we walk on the previously forbidden part of the beach, I stop to take a photo of one of my goddess figurines on a piece of faded green driftwood. I am in that state of total presence that I experience often in our island walks, the complete immersion in the moment, stripped of all other purpose or task, but simply myself, walking on the beach. It is a type of what I call *stepping through,* as if I have stepped out of myself, out of reality, and into a different plane of relationship with the natural world.

We find several fighting conch shells fairly close together and I say to my husband: *what we really need to do is find where the moon snails come up.* I turn away from the driftwood to continue walking and just as his foot begins to come down on the sand I see it...right below where his foot is poised to step, the distinctive curve of a huge moon snail shell, half-buried in the sand. I grab his arm and pull him back, making an indistinct babbling sort of squeal in my throat. I dig it up and there It Is, a sun-bleached moon snail shell that exactly fills the palm of my hand. I laugh with joy and exhilaration and nearly cry in my delight. I tell my husband I feel as excited and happy and full of wild euphoria as if I've just given birth to another child. *This is one of the best moments of my life!* I crow, laughing semi-hysterically, *this ranks right up there with the time we saw the otters at the river!*

Then, realizing what I have said, I laugh some more. Is it sad, perhaps even pathetic, that some of the best moments of my life have been seeing wild otters and finding perfect shells? No, I decide, I adore being the kind of person who sees with island eyes and who discovers the best moments of her life simply by paying attention to what is happening on the shore.

At its best, working and schooling from home with our family of six feels like a beautifully seamless integration of work and life—there is no need to compartmentalize or draw distinctions between life and work, because it is ALL just *life and living*. At its worst, it feels like the work bleeds into everything else in an all-consuming way and the to-do list just never ends and something or someone is always getting overlooked or shortchanged. We find that it is helpful for us all sometimes to just all step away and be somewhere else, while the to-do list stays at home! We try to take at least five family adventures a year and in the spring after our long beach trip, we took a short mini vacation about three hours away to Table Rock Lake.

One morning on this lake vacation, I went for a walk with our youngest son, Tanner (then three), to collect supplies for a goddess grid. As we came up the steps near our room, we discovered that there were many different sizes of snails crawling along the rain-dampened stone steps. Tanner exclaimed, *it's a wild snail festival out here!* and squatted down to admire the snails. I crouched and admired the snails with him, watching them slowly investigate the goddess figurine I'd set on the steps and reflected that if we hadn't made the time to squat down, to get to a snail's eye level, we would never have seen them. *I loved it.* I loved the rhythm of this "wild snail festival." He meant wild in the sense of "crazy party" rather than "opposite of domestic" and I loved his choice of wording.

How beautifully incongruous and wonderful it was to think of "snail" and "festival" or "snail" and "wild" in the same context and it felt like this charming moment, time out of time, just partying with the wild snails.

When we returned from the beach, I also reinstated my daily "woodspriestess" practice: visiting the same spot on the big rocks in the woods behind my house every day, rain or shine, without fail, and seeing what I learn from the woods, the world, and myself. It is vital to my well-being. After maintaining this daily practice for two years prior to the birth of our fourth child, I let my dedication slip. This year, each morning I again awoke with a sense of excitement and anticipation to see what I will discover. This simple act of connection re-enchanted my daily world and more deeply connected me to an undercurrent of everyday magic running through my life. Over the course of the year, the collection of poems included in this book emerged as a direct result of devoted, daily time in the woods. Many of these moments may seem small or insignificant, but this is the gift—to delight in the small bits of everyday magic woven through our world.

In one of my favorite books, *Listening to the Oracle*, Diane Skafte writes:

Ancient people saw and heard oracles everywhere because they lived in an ensouled world. The phrase 'ensouled world' may inspire us today, but perceiving everything around us as truly alive, brimming with consciousness, intensely present, and gazing back at us is an experience of a different order. Few adults living in modern culture are able to sustain an ensouled relationship with creation for more than a few moments at a time...

In the woods one morning, back at home from both beach and lake, I laid on my back on the rocks, stuck my legs straight up in the air and then spread them open to the sky. I brought my knees into my chest and laid there on the stone like a stranded beetle for a while thinking.

I had the sensation that I was waiting for something, some insight or inspiration or magical something to happen, and I had a vague feeling of disappointment in such a "normal day" with no special lesson or encounter.

But, then I heard a small voice from within say:

Well, you got your spirit back, so there's that.

And, I decided that was enough.

On my way back to the house, right in my path, there was a snail on a leaf.

**May we always
have time
to take part
in wild snail festivals.**

She Lives Her Poems

She plucks cedar from her hair
empties berries
from the folds of her shirt
carries a goddess in her pocket.
Finds spiral shells
in stone, beach, and thicket.
Listens to messages from her soul
on wings of crows
and wisps of air.
Prays in flowers
and to flowers.
Stands barefoot
on limestone and moss
to offer blessings
to the wide sky.
She lives her poems.

Winter

How to Discover the Meaning of Life

Find a rock
beside an open stream
Or a piece of driftwood
beside the ocean
Or even a tree
beside the highway

Sit.
Sit with yourself
Sit with the air.
Look for a bird.
Feel your heart beat
in your wrist.

Watch the sky
become pink
And as you somersault
backward into the night
Smile.

Brigid's Invocation

I stand in the center of the wheel, Brigid,
and I ask for your wisdom,
your guidance, and your blessing.

I turn to the East and call it in.
Cool air.
Fresh breath of wisdom.
A sigh of release and freedom.
The whisper of poetry on the wind.

I turn to South and call it in.
The brightness of new ideas.
The warmth of the sun.
The fiery forge of transformation.
The heat of my own skin.

I turn to the West and call it in.
The patter of rainfall.
The sweep of the river.
The healing waters of her well.
The swift hum of blood in my veins.

I turn to the North and call it in.
The solidness of stone.
The grand arc of the trees against the sky.

The steady heart of the sacred oak.
The anchoring of my own feet
on this beautiful ground.

A Greeting from the Past

*Something about the way
light catches on the pier
brings a remembrance
of an earlier age
priestesses on temple steps
arms lifted to the sky
power held with easy grace
rippling through fingertips
across, through, and within
ribbons of time.
A greeting
from long before
this day.*

Hope on the Waves

I will walk with you
at the edge of the world
offering hope on the waves
whispering prayers on the winds
and sending the deepest wishes
of our united hearts
to the joining
of sea, shore, and sky.

Imbolc Magic

Listen.
I tell of prayers
strung through oak leaves.
Deep wells,
emerald fields,
hot coals.
I know the courage it takes
to tend the flame
of ancient mystery.

Brigid Invocation (song)

Healing water
Sacred flame
Brigid we
invoke your name

Holy fire
Sacred water(s)
Honored one
I (we) am (are) your daughter(s)

Breath of life
Ancient earth
Upon your hearth
I claim my worth

Living earth
Blessed breath
In your hands
through life and death

Sacred touch
Holy hour(s)
In this space
we feel your power(s)

Healing water
Sacred flame
Breath of air
we call your name.

Inner Flame

This morning
dawned through
bare trees
and icy logs.
I listened to the crows call
watched the cats twine
through the woodpile
and heard a deer picking her way
through the stones.
The air was sharp with cold,
but I felt lit with a fire
from without and within.

A No Pressure Prayer for Today

May I hold
my center
May I keep
my own counsel
May I trust
my heart.

Yes, Please

The way the climbing sunlight
strikes the stones
almost makes it feel
like they were placed there on purpose
to be a perfect sunrise sitting spot.
I stood there listening to
a morning chorus
composed of crow,
woodpecker, and rooster
with notes of songbird
and rustle of squirrel
and only two words
were in my mind:

Yes, please.

Finding Poems

I am finding poems again
waiting for me in the woods
nestled in curve of stone
carried on sweet breezes
and in the notes of wind
and woodpecker
scattered through oak leaves
and curling through lichen,
moss, and branch.

I am finding poems again
and with them, myself.

The Body of the Goddess

*I stand on the body
of the Goddess
I sit on her bones
I breathe with her breeze
the veins in my arms
tracing the patterns of rivers
to the sea
the fiery pulse at my center
matching the heat of her core
beneath wakening soil.
I lie back
in the palm of her hand
and watch the sky.*

What is Now

In listening
to a symphony
composed of
birchbark
cardinal feather
and fungus,
She rises from
what has broken
and embraces
what is now.

What Remains

It can be easy
to romanticize nature
and the teachings
of Gaia.
It is hard to keep going
when your petals
are twisted and blackened
when ice has settled
in the cells of your heart
and burst your core.
And yet, still opening
what remains of yourself
to the sun
and blooming
with everything
you've got left.

Malta

I am heartsong
and hearthsong
a voice lifted in exultant praise
in hilltop temple
and in the quiet whispers
of sacred chambers
and secret dreams.

I have dreamed myself back
from the temples of old
and I listen to
soulprayer
hearthwisdom
flamekeeping
heartholding
and hope.

Spring

Sunrise Prayer

I open my hands to this new day.
I open my heart to this new day.
I open my hopes to this new day.
May it be blessed.

Wild Secrets

Listen for
wild secrets
in the place
where pine
shares mysteries
with palm.

Spring Whispers

Spring is whispering
to cave water
emerging through mossy stone
and to violet leaf nestled
in curve of root
waiting for a
sunlight kiss
to bloom.

Prayer at Sunrise

May I be open to magic in all of its
wild, mysterious, surprising, and beautiful
forms.
May my heart be light
and may my shoulders soften easily.
May I have no fear of my own power
and may I walk through my other fears with
courage.
May I live, laugh, and love with awareness
and may I experience this day
wisely, wonderfully, and well.

Touching the Infinite

My only prayer
today
is to touch
the infinite.

Support

It is a beautiful day.
It is a beautiful world.
There is beautiful work to do.
You don't have to hold everything.
You are supported.
You are supported.
You are supported.
Remember to source
from the support around you
rather than drawing
all your power from your own core.

Welcoming Spring

Arise!
Let us greet this morning
with smiling faces
Hair unbound
Hearts full of glee
Birdsong in one hand
Roses in the other
Let us dance to River's music
And Earth's heartbeat
Under quickening leaves
We are full with the promise of spring.

Ostara Magic

Listen.
I am the whisper of iris
the violet's kiss
the leaf's song
from tight within the bud
I blossom
into my magic.

Dogwood Song

Standing on steep hillsides,
leaning from rocky patches of ground,
roots feeling deep in the dark,
searching for the nourishment
that is only possible in shadowed places.
Raindrop blessing
petal and leaf.
Sunlight filtered through a canopy of oaks.
Branches spreading graciously.
A living love song
strung through the woods like lace.

A Spring Self-Blessing

May you know the tenacity of serviceberry
the grace of dogwood
the heart of plum
and the ferocity of raspberry.
May you have the wisdom to know
when to flow like the river
and when to stand like the mountain.
May you dance with the rain
allow your thunder to be heard
smile with the radiance of the sun
and may you know you walk
in the hand of the goddess
all the days of your life.

Sound and Silence

This morning
birdsong filled the air
in a patterned chorus
raised above the grinding notes
of distant trucks on the highway.
Through it all,
a surprisingly distinct sound
the rasping dance
of two dry leaves
twining around one another
high on a branch
somehow differentiated
from all else
as a unique note
in the symphony.

I laid on my back on the rock
and looked up at the white clouds,
still against the morning sky
and black branches,
and felt between
sound
and silence.

Magic Everywhere

The mist hanging
in the valley
traces the line of
flooded creek.
The maple buds
red against blue sky.
The earth exhales a
slow breath under
saturated ground.
Crouching beneath cedar's arms
studying the stained-glass effect
of sunlight through oak leaves
two things are clear:
there are stories
in the smallest places
there is magic
everywhere.

Beltane Magic

Listen
I tell of the ephemeral
and fleeting
the persistent
renewal of beauty.
The wild enchantment
you feel whispering
through your veins.
The love songs
of the earth.
The sparkles of sunlight
on blossom
and in hearts.
I am radiant.

Beltane Moon

I didn't just stop
to smell the lilacs
I sang to them too
praising their beauty
as I pressed my nose
into their blooms.

The air was full
of enchantment
as I delighted in the sunlight
filtered through new maple leaves
and scattered across stone.

I rolled redbud flowers
across my tongue
and ate dandelions straight
from the stem
feeling yellow petals
in my teeth.

I savored the flavor of a violet
and rubbed mint leaves
between my fingers
I crawled on my knees
through the clover

watched bees dance
on the dandelions
and found ginger
and elderberry beneath
my heels as I stretched
my arms into a tree branch
reaching for tender buds.

I gathered the blossoms
of springtime
kissed them with gratitude
and offered them into
the bubbles of water
from which rivers are born.

I let my fingers trail
through the wildness
within me and around me.

Then I lifted my lips
to my lover
under the
Beltane moon.

May Morning

I woke with the smell
of Belfire still in my hair
and knelt in a circle
of hawthorn and roses
to bless my brow, cheeks,
and neck with dew.
I heard the sound of
hooves on leaf and stone
and saw three deer leaping
away through the woods.
I lifted my arms to sun
exhilarated with wild enchantment.
What a blessing it is to live
right here, right now.

Good May Morning!

Maple Quest

*I followed a quest
from sun on
dogwood blossom
to light through maple leaf
and discovered that
the brambles I tried to uproot
in January
are actually wild raspberries
twining up through stone.
A heroine's journey
of the smallest
and most significant
kind.*

New Moon

We honor the new moon
and her blessings.
Letting go, releasing, shedding.
That which no longer serves
is gently released
That which is desired,
slips out into the crack of possibility
and takes root,
preparing to grow.

But, for now a moment to rest.
To keep silent peace.
To soak in the dark of the moon
and her promise of quiet

deep
renewal.

Azores

I listen
to the taste of roses,
hidden wisdom
and that which is
shrouded in secrecy.
I have danced in meadows
blanketed with flowers,
howled in the shadows,
listened to the river,
and sung to the stars in the night.
I ask you to attend
to the mystery
and to have faith that
you hold the key
to your own awakening.

Summer

Caring About It

I had a conversation
with myself in the woods
this morning
first marveling
at the privilege of
bearing witness to so many
changes in one small space
and remembering
the moments in which
light made stained glass
of the leaf-strewn ground
and the time when small canopies
of newborn maple leaves
captivated me with their glow.
Feeling full of gratitude,
appreciation for just paying attention
I said aloud:
"Oh, how much I would have missed!"
Another part of me said:
"I suppose...if what you care about
is the way dew rests on
maple leaves and raspberries."
But, in fact, I do care

and I swiped my finger
across the leaves
anointed my face
with dewdrops
and smiled in the sun.

Inanna Speaks

Inanna speaks
she says
it is time
to step into
the heart of mystery
to set foot
on the path of wild wisdom
to journey to the very depths
of your core.

And once you have descended
deep into the underworld
into the place where
pain and power meet
in the crucible of your life

once you are laid bare
stripped raw
and shaking in your bones
you will discover
there is nothing left to fear
there is nothing left to do
there is no one left to please.

You will taste this freedom
in the salt of blood
and the sweetness of wild berries
and then you will turn
naked
unapologetic
and unafraid,
put your feet upon the path
perhaps still unknown,
but unfolding before you
and you will ascend
through the layers
of that which you no longer need
through the roles that you
no longer inhabit
through the wants that you
no longer fulfill.

You will reclaim your
staff of power
you will accept your
cape of mystery
and you will emerge
from the underworld
with something fierce
blazing in your eyes.

And in the set of your shoulders
and the swirl of your hips
there is something
that can no longer be denied.

You will emerge.
Whole.

Rose Wisdom

They tried to graft other
lives to mine
knowing I was of sturdy stock
persistent, resistant, capable.
After feeding on my strength
and using my resources
that which was grafted
fell away
and only my own, small,
devoted beauty
remained to reach wildhearted
for the sun.

Dandelion Lesson

Dandelion lesson.
Summer's herald
smells like rain
and honey
and hope.
Blood tonic.
Liver support.
Dance of determination
and refusal.
Listen.
She whispers of the hive,
of humbleness, and healing.

A Web of Remembrance

I believe there are places
where roses remember raindrops
and the taste of sun.
Berries remember the rooting
of canes in earth.
Milkweed remembers the feet
of butterflies.
Oak branches remember
the delicate weight of wren.
And stones
remember the long-ago
touch of the sea.
Perhaps the breeze remembers October
and the skies the sound of thunder.
Perhaps we all weave a web of remembrance
that stitches the world together.

Wildberry Yoga

I practiced wildberry yoga today
accompanied by a playlist of thunder
and the fairy footsteps of raindrops
on raspberry leaves.
A little extension of the rib cage
yields the best fruit.
Yielding to tight spaces
feeling prickles of discomfort
and yet
leaning in a little deeper
to get a good stretch.
Reaching an arm to the right
and then sweeping across
the body to the left.
Extending down to the toes
and then, up, up, up...
hold it for a moment.
And in nameless green moments
of discovery
make contact with the soul.

Original Sacrament

From sunlight and rain
into root and berry
into body and blood.
A sacrament
a communion
a celebration.

Getting My Spirit Back

This morning
I laid on my back on the rocks
stuck my legs straight up in the air
and then spread them open to the sky.

I brought my knees into my chest
and laid there on the stone
like a stranded beetle for a while
thinking.

I had the sensation
that I was waiting for something,
some insight or
inspiration or
magical something
to happen,
and had a vague feeling
of disappointment
in such a "normal day"
with no special lesson
or encounter.

But, then I heard a small voice
from within say:

"well, you got your spirit back,
so there's that."

And, I decided that was enough.

On my way back to the house,
there was a snail on a leaf.

Kneeling

One day you may kneel
in a patch of moss
beside a cedar
and as a mourning dove
flies over head
discover that
you understand everything
and...or
you understand nothing
and both of these
feel fine.

Rose Prayers

She prays
hopes
and heals
in roses.
This is the season
for rose prayers.
Witnessing
celebrating,
honoring,
offering.

This Can Be Summer

I watched a brilliant green snake
twine sinuously through an ash tree
moving with such skillful grace
across the branches
it almost became invisible
in the dappled
emerald shadows.

I felt the sun soak into my skin
picking wild raspberries
with sweat shining my shoulders.

I sank into ice-cold water,
where the earth gives
birth to the river.

I gathered a handful
of rose petals
and stood facing the horizon
considering the possible.

This can be summer
liquid

languorous
luminous.

Sisters Past

I hear a whisper
from ages past
an echo of footfalls
on temple steps.
Glad voices lift
with river's song.
Arms reach toward
summer's sun.
I feel the brush
of sisters past
speaking in
an ancient silence.

Everyday Moonboat

Sometimes the Moonboat
journeys
into mysteries of mulberry
and raspberry wilds
the countless irrepressible
tiny adventures,
magic,
heart and hope,
of small spaces
and everyday places.

Fairy Dance

I watched fairies dance
in the midsummer twilight
waltzing with fireflies
and skimming through treetops.
It is true that they could have
been moths,
but as I stood in the shadows
with my children
all of us gazing upward in wonder
the sky deepening to night
I saw the certainty shining
in their faces,
the enchantment in their eyes
and I knew
without a doubt
that we were seeing the true nature
of these winged creatures.
And we will never forget what
it felt like to watch
real fairies taking flight
right before us
as we dared to name
the magic in the night.

Coyote Eyes

I became aware
that I was not alone in the woods.
Sitting on the rocks, I looked through
the leaves to come eye to eye
with a coyote,
sitting in a direct line across from me,
apparently also enjoying
the cool morning air
and heavy greenness of the trees.

We exchanged glances
we sniffed the air.
We sat still and looked.
After what felt like a timeless
experience of companionable stillness,
an interspecies appreciation of the
same terrain
we both got up
and went our own ways.

May we always remember
to share vision
with eyes of the wild.

The River of Your Life

*What if you were to sit
by the river of your own life
observing the current
watching the flow,
sensing the depth,
feeling the rhythm,
and not needing
to tell about it,
but instead taking
a long, replenishing
drink.*

A Bath

This morning
I bathed
in birdsong
wind
and wholeness.

Presence

Inhale
exhale
greet the day
with presence
and a tender heart.

Fierce Fruit

Attend to the seeds
of the wild
for they reveal
fierce and holy
fruit.

Awareness Chant

I am awake.
I am aware.
I am alive
alive
alive.

Litha Magic

Listen.
I am summer's song
the sweet blessing of water's flow
the exuberant reach of blossoms
for the sun.
The dance of sunlight and shadow
through white clouds
and radiant growth.

Summer Love

Too busy. Too buzzy.
Not enough time.
To do. To do. To do.
Scramble. Hurry.
Tight chest
Tight breath
Tight heart
WAIT!
Listen to Summer.
Languid. Warm. Sweaty. Hot.
Petals soften
Juice drips
Kissed by sunlight
Bathed with rain
Sweet stickiness.
Passion.
Summer is heavy.
Hot and ready.
Blooming and dripping.
Unfolding.
Becoming.
Ripening.
Sweet. Tangy. Biting.

Feel it in the air.
Greet it at sunset.
Throw your arms around it.
Dig in. Hang on. This is IT.
Taste it. Hold it. Enfold it. Be it.
Lick it. Know it. Be it. Embrace it.
This is your life.
*This is **your life.***
Do you love it?

Listening

Sometimes neither words
nor photo can explain
the way the sun shines through
the branches
and a pocket of mist rises
from wet ground
giving the impression
that there is a enchanted path
leading off through the trees.

If you follow this path,
you will marvel
at the way raindrops hang heavy
from grateful branches
and how a tiny rainbow is captured
in just one.

You will wonder at the spangled
spiderwebs jeweled across the way
holding patience
and a watchful appetite.

Breathing in the

greenness
with cedar spiking the top of your head,
webs tangling your arms,
and gratitude softening your heart
and eyes
the questions of living fade away
and there is only you

listening.

Spider Wisdom

Today it was sunlight
on a spiderweb
that threaded enchantment
through the morning.
Tend to the
weaving of your life.
Create with intention.
Feel
the sun sparkles
on the path.

I'm Listening

Today smells like roses,
tastes like blackberries,
sounds like raindrops,
and looks like gratitude.
I'm listening.

Three Crows

I was sitting on the deck,
pining for the woods
and feeling cut off from my source.
I watched some yellow leaves
twirling down from the trees
and admired the last of the blackberries.
I put my hand on my heart
and took some deep breaths.
I heard a sound from the woods,
above the rocks where I usually sit,
and three crows flew up
and arced across the sky
in succession above my head.
As I smiled with relief and gratitude,
I felt again that sensation of magic
that fuels my soul every day.

Maple Leaves

I watched these maple leaves
be born in the spring.
Tender green scrolls
tilting towards the earth
like folded umbrellas
and, through raindrop
and sunlight, first
opening halfway into
perfect little canopies
to catch the light
in a way that lit the woods
and captivated my attention.
In later spring
spreading five fingers wide open
each capable of holding a raindrop
and filtering the light
to a soft green haze.
And, now, a drought.

If it was already fall,
they would be beautiful,
but in truth they are parched.
Yellow, brittle-edged, dry
and curled, a few

twisting through the air
to alight on thirsty ground.

My words, and thoughts too,
feel parched and brittle
and yet still, this light
through these leaves
continues to enchant me.

Named and Numinous

Today I watched a red bird
with black wings
sit on a branch
and an orange butterfly
rest on a rock.
There is magic to be found
in both the named
and the numinous.

Lammas Magic

Listen.
My heart overflows with abundance
and gratitude.
I know the magic
of golden kernel
plump berry
rich ground.
The symphony of wheat and corn
And what it feels like to
dance sunlight into wine.

Iona

I listen at the edge of
wave song
on sacred shores
I am the sigh of the tide,
the swell of the moon,
the wild rhythm of the earth.
There is so much to know.

Pause.
Wait.
Breathe.

I hold an open space
in my heart
I take a deep breath
I lift my face towards the sun
and
I listen.

Autumn

Juncture

At the juncture of
sunlight and shadow,
sound and silence,
darkness and dawn,
drought and rainfall.
Summer and autumn
are holding quiet
meetings in the woods.

September Roses

I have returned from admiring
sunrise through cedar,
gathering September rose petals
while my mind dances with
images of moon-crowned women
by the firelight
and strains of melodies
from ceremonies past
twine through the air,
ready to be remembered.
One part of me moves
to hurry indoors because
the to-do list is long
but I stand barefoot
in the dewy grass
with sunlight across my eyelids
for a while longer
because this, too,
is everything.

Drifting Prayers

Oh, holy, holy
these prayers that drift
on falling leaves
and wisps of cloud
dropping into my
cupped hands
with my dreams.

Stories Worth Telling

There are opportunities
to listen
everywhere.
The meeting of
root with creekbank.
The conversation
between oak and slate.
The dance of
day with dusk.
These are stories
worth telling.

Prayer for a Busy Day

May I be tender with my heart
and hold myself with compassion.
May I guard my soft interior
with grace and determination
May my footsteps be gentle
May my hands be open
May my shoulders soften
and may this sweet breeze
of morning
teach me how to flow.

Crone Blessing

May she be reminded of
the unfurling braid of her own life
the sacred weaving
she tends to with care
the work she has done
and that is yet to come.

In this braid may she hear
the whispers of a new story
the singing of her own song
where she's been
and where she's going.
and may she remember
her own power
to pull the disparate threads
of her life together
and to view them as one
beautiful whole.

May she walk in love.
May she walk in beauty.
May she walk with trust.
May she walk with courage.
May it be so.

Mushroom Morning

This morning I encountered
the glistening face
of a newly born mushroom
by a rock.

Then, I hoisted my youngest child
onto my hip and marveled
at the miracle of carrying built-in
seats for children
wherever I go.

This is my news today.

Harvest Magic

Listen.
I am autumn's song
the gentle drift of falling leaves
the wisdom of letting go

I tell of the rapt engagement
of the harvest moon
the howl of wolf
the glow of firelight
harvest's gifts tumbling
into grateful hands.

In the whispers of the wind
and the ember-glow
of contemplation
I smile
with gratitude.

Mabon Magic

Listen.
I am steeping in my wisdom
Stirring up my spirit
Savoring my flavor.
I am twilight
and shadow.
Deepen with me
and become the container
of your own emergence...

Sunlight and Shadow

I want to live
my life
allowing space
to watch
sunlight and shadow
move to center.

Deepening Prayer

May I deepen now
deepen into twilight
deepen into myself.
May I deepen into silence
deepen into shadow
deepen into the sacred.
May I deepen
into stillness.
May I soften.
May I quiet my heart
and may I listen.
May I deepen
so that I might become
the container
for my own emergence.

Hearthfire

Listen.
I know the mysteries
of the deepwood
the whisper of forest within acorn
the fleeting enchantment
of an October rose.
Dance with me
in hearthfire
and fallen leaves.

Hecate of the Three Ways

She who shows her incisors
She who midwifes death
She who illuminates the crossroads.

She who gathers and releases
She who creates and destroys.
She who covers and reveals.

She is the darkness and the light within it.
She is the crossroads and the path.
She is the guardian and the wayshower

before her and behind her
is the knowing unknown.

Blessing from the Harvest Queen

May the sunset cloak
of shorter days enfold you
May you dance with the patterns
of crimson and gold leaves
May you sing with owl and coyote
in crisp moonlight
May you savor the orangeness
of pumpkin and yam
and feel the sweetness
of honey on your tongue.
May you listen to the dreams of seed corn
May elderberry strengthen you
with stored sunshine
May persimmon grant you
a fleeting hello
May the poignant flare
of an October rose
kiss you with hope.
May your rooms be
wreathed with smiles.
And, may you remember
the grace and wisdom
found in both
gathering and releasing.

Samhain Magic

Listen.
The veil is thin.
I spin the web.
I call the circle.
I honor the ancestors.
I am she who
weaves the whole
She who
holds the all
She who
knows the
pattern of the ages.

Braiding Life

What do you do when you feel so frayed
as if the very fibers of yourself are unraveling
into nothing?

You gather your fragments tenderly
coax them back from where they have
wandered
unwind them from their hiding places
gather them together into your cupped hands.

Look at this rainbow of your life
some lumpy and bumpy
some fine and graceful
some bright and colorful
some gray and threadbare.

We all have rough places in the weaving of life
we all have moments when our colors feel
faded
and wrung out.

Sometimes the only thing to do is look
and listen
and wait

And, then, when the time is right
gather together those soft threads of your
existence
smooth your hands over them
even the parts that feel knobby
clasp them to your heart with
tenderness
gratitude and appreciation
and then
begin
to braid
them together.

Raindrops

Today I walked
through spiderwebs
rain slicked stone
and damp moss
to discover
this yellow leaf on a stone
a perfect cup
for raindrops.

Rise

*Let us rise today
with hearts full of courage
hands full of compassion
and arms full of hope.*

Beyond

*Where sea oats nod
and sailboats sway.
At the edge of beyond
today.*

Wishes

I stood by the ocean
and watched
an eagle and an osprey
dance in the sky.
I tasted salt on my skin
and felt ease in the air.
I listened to the waves
and to my wishes
coming true.

Ocean Morning Prayer

May I rise today with strength
and an open heart.
May my shoulders soften
with the release of expectation.
May my thoughts clear
with the sky.
May my edges round
as I move with the tides.
May I accept the ebb and flow of life.
May I be exquisitely alert to what is.
And, may I feel the soft breath
of inspiration
on the wind.

Feeling My Magic

What do I need to feel my magic?
This was the question that floated to my mind
in the woods this morning
but it could also be about feeding my magic or
fueling my magic...

I need
time alone with my soul
and with the sun
blank pages
and open spaces
sunlight on cedar
and moonlight
over a broad field.
Bare feet
on stone
or sand.
Time to join hands
with another
and to be in solitude.
The opportunity
to move my body
extend my limits

and to lift my arms
to the sky.
To touch the earth
to feel my heartbeat
and to watch the weaving
of the world
unfurling before my eyes.

Winter Again

Requiem for a Tree

When they logged this hillside
one hundred years ago
they left you standing sentinel.

I'm not sure why
you were spared above the others
perhaps it is the way you stand above
the rocks
looking out across the horizon
like a guardian.

Perhaps they felt the same pulse
beneath your bark
that I felt when I first laid
my hands upon you and whispered
my question.

Grandfather Tree,
I called you.
Something definitively wise
in stature
girth
and sweep of branches.

I watched those branches bud
and leaf each spring
and noted when some branches
began to fail to leaf.

Five times bigger than any tree
for many acres
you commanded attention
even when some of your branches
began to drop in heavy fall winds.

One winter, during my thirty-fifth year
a raccoon poked its head
out of your trunk
and told me I was pregnant.

It was true
and as I came to welcome
the new babe
within
I also knew that your trunk
was becoming
hollow
and your years left were few.

I saw your final branch fall last year

and today, noticed
that you have released the top half
of your massive trunk.

You bore witness to more
life and changes on this hillside
than any other single life form
ever will.

In a hollow of a large knot
a puddle of rainwater
makes a dish from which my dog drinks.
Moss rings your trunk
and a panoply of mushrooms
blossoms
from fallen limbs
and bark.

I explored the crevices of your
remains with awe
feeling as if I'd stepped into
another world
where whorl, and fungus,
shadow and sunlight
and crumble of oak leaf

are the only things that matter.
I kissed a handful of rose petals
laid them at your base
and said thank you.

It isn't goodbye.
There is much left to learn.

Dreamtime

A wisdom whispers
from the Dreamtime
calling me to ceremony and song
it flickers in the firelight
of ancient memory
rippling along my spine
dancing through my fingertips.

What is it that calls me in the night?
I look up
She's pouring tea across from me
a patterned rhythm to her movements
that speaks
of sacred knowing.

A door opens
She is ready to share
and yet, I slip away
through the undercurrents of time
falling down out of space
out of memory
out of song
and out of touch.

Landing
in a soft bed
my arm curled around my
nursling
hearing his breath in the dark
and wondering
what I am missing
what I'm forgetting
and what remembering
is right here.

Avalon

I am a wisdomkeeper
wayknower
and heart-tender.
I listen to the white moon
above the Tor
the whisper of the mists
and the flutter of wings
across gentle waters.
The guardians of temples old
speak through me
and call your name.

Children of Wonder

She who cannot be contained.
She who knows no end.
She who holds all things.

Behold that which is new and ever-changing.
Behold that which is ancient and unyielding.
Behold that which is meant for you
and that which is meant to come from you.

Behold the tapestry of life being woven before you.
Receive her kiss.
Feel her embrace.
And walk in peace and prayer.

Yule Magic

Listen.
I am the sound of snowfall
on quiet ground
I speak of the cycles of change
the rhythms of the earth
the clear potential of a new year
and the wisdom of your soul.

Solstice Night

Listen.
I speak of deep places.
The wisdom of endarkenment.
The womenergy that spins cells
into souls
into being.
This is our sacred path.
A woman's journey to herself.

Winter Magic

Listen.
I am winter's song
the gentle drift of falling snow
the wisdom of incubation
and hibernation
the wonder and magic
of cave time.
I tell of the howl of wolf
the glow of firelight
the bright, cool light
of a midnight moon
winter's gifts tumbling
into grateful hands.
In the whispers of the wind
the bite of cold,
the ember-glow
of contemplation,
I find the secrets
of my self
and soul.

Elen

Listen.
I guide the Ways.
My mysteries chime in the night.
Wait for the dreamtime.
And walk with me between trees
and worlds.

Skadi

Listen.
My aim is true.
I tell of winter's shadow
across the land
the wild whirl of cold
the quickening of the hunt
a sharpness that sings
of both icicle and talon.

Mother Winter (Holda)

Listen.
I spin my magic
through snowflake
and icicle
I summon the winter's wild
and blanket those in need
with comfort.

Mother Winter (Caireen)

Listen.
I spin protection
through green hills
and winter's chills.
I summon the power of the wild
and blanket those in need
with comfort.

Waiting for a Poem

I don't feel a poem today
they usually arrive with
a graceful whisper
some touch of the light on a leaf
triggering the exact word
the unfolding of a series
of small moments
into a story that asks to be heard
expressed
birthed into being
shared.

Sometimes they dance
around the edges of my
consciousness
a word lands

then a bird
there above me
bringing the message home.

Raindrops catch in spiderweb
a leaf drops from the sky to touch
my back
an acorn is discovered

resting on a rock
a mushroom peeks up
from beneath dry leaves
or a sweet raspberry nestles
in the curve of a vine

And, in those moments
I know I've found my poem.

I wait for them to find me
and when they do
I smile to receive the gift
and I delight in
the living of my poems.

Daily Prayer (two versions)

Original:

Goddess,
I am open to your power
I am open to your presence
I am open to your peace
Help me to know that I walk
in the palm of your hand
today and forever
blessed be and thank you.

Expanded edition:

Goddess,
I am open to your power
I am open to your presence
I am open to your peace
I am open to your plan.
I am open to your passion
I am open to your plenty
I am open to your pleasure
I am open to your patience.
I am open to your possibility.

I am open to your purpose
I am open to your path.
Help me to know that I walk
in the palm of your hand
today and forever
blessed be and thank you.

Chants

Summer Peace Chant

Peace
Power
Passion
and Plenty.

Part Fire, Part Dream

Part fire
part dream
I am the seer
and the unseen.

I am Powerful

I am powerful
I am magical
I am healthy
I am free.

I am Listening

I am listening
I am opening
I am learning
I am free.

Body Prayer

My body is my altar,
My body is my temple,
My living presence on this earth,
My prayer, my prayer, my prayer.

The Great Return

Scatter my ashes on
the tree covered hills
Let my bones come
to rest on these stones
Raindrops will come
to carry me away
Back to the
Fire of All.

Moon Wise

(composed with kids)
Moon wise woman
Moon wise baby
We are moon wise
We are moon wise.
Yeah, yeah, yeah!

The Goddess in Us
(collaborative with five year old daughter)

I see the goddess in the moon
I feel the goddess in the earth
I taste the goddess in the wind
I hear the goddess in my heart
I touch the goddess in your hand.

Song in the Dark

Darkness falls
Darkness enfolds
Darkness calls
Darkness holds
Hallowed evening
Hallowed night
We rest in the shadows
We offer our light.

Crescent Moon Song

I walk the crescent moon
Plant the seeds and wait to bloom.
I dance the crescent moon
Change is coming, making room.
I sing the crescent moon
Weave intention with her loom.

Power Song
(collaborative with kids)

We feel the power of our hearts.
We feel the power of our minds.
We feel the power of our bodies.
We feel the power of our family.
We feel the power of our drum.
We feel the power.
We feel the power.
We feel the power!

May it Flow

May it flow.
May we grow.
May it be so.

Beauty All Around

Even broken
even bound
there is beauty
all around.

Release

*I release myself
to the power of
what is
right now.*

Exploring the mysteries
of time and space
soul and place.

Come join the Circle!

Membership in the Creative Spirit Circle is FREE and packed with beautiful, bountiful resources, including:

- a free Womanrunes e-course
- Goddess Studies and Ritual course
- additional seasonal e-courses
- weekly virtual circles in our Facebook group
- Red Tent, sacred ceremony, and ritual resources
- goddess mandalas
- access to Divine Imperfections sculptures at discounted prices
- monthly *Creative Spirit Circle Journal* filled with resources such as ceremony outlines, articles, book recommendations, sneak peeks, and special freebies.

Claim your place in the Circle:
brigidsgrove.com/come-join-the-circle

Molly also writes regularly at the Brigid's Grove Patreon, where multiple tiers of membership include monthly goddess magic mail: patreon.com/brigidsgrove

Connect with Brigid's Grove:

- brigidsgrove.com
- facebook.com/brigidsgrove
- patreon.com/brigidsgrove
- instagram.com/brigidsgrove
- brigidsgrove.etsy.com
- Creative Spirit Circle Facebook Group: facebook.com/groups/ brigidsgrovecreativespiritcircle

About the Author:

Molly has been gathering the women to circle, sing, celebrate, and share since 2008. She plans and facilitates women's circles, Red Tents, seasonal retreats and rituals, Pink Tent mother-daughter circles, and family ceremonies in rural Missouri and

teaches online courses in Red Tent facilitation and Practical Priestessing.

Molly is a priestess who holds MSW, M.Div, and D.Min degrees and wrote her dissertation about contemporary priestessing in the U.S.

Molly is the author of *Womanrunes*, *Earthprayer*, and *The Red Tent Resource Kit*. She writes about women's circles, nature, practical priestessing, creativity, family ritual, and the goddess at Brigid's Grove, SageWoman Magazine, and Feminism and Religion.

About Brigid's Grove:

Molly and Mark co-
create original Story
Goddesses, goddess
sculptures, mini goddess
pendants, and ceremony
kits at
brigidsgrove.etsy.com.
They publish
Womanrunes books and
decks, based on the
work of Shekhinah
Mountainwater.

Brigid's Grove integrates Molly's priestess
work and goddess studies with our family's
shared interests in ceremony, art, gemstones,
metalwork, nature, and intentional, creative
living.

Brigid is the Irish triple goddess of smithcraft,
poetry, and midwifery. She is also a Christian
saint associated with midwives, birthing
mothers, and infants.